P9-BZG-229

The Way of Water

John —

Good luck to you in your freedom of retirement.

Your friend,

Michael Ricca

The Way of Water

Perch Mountain Poems
2002—2012

Michael Riedell

.

SLOW
MOUNTAIN
PRESS

Some of the poems in this collection originally appeared in somewhat different form in the following publications: *Edgz, Greenfuse, The Orange Room Review*, and the anthologies, *Small Mirrors* and *No Food or Drink*.

Copyright © 2014 by Michael Riedell

All rights reserved. No part of this book may be reproduced, scanned, or distributed in any printed or electronic form without permission from the publisher, except by a reviewer, who may quote brief passages in a review.

9 8 7 6 5 4 3 2 1

First Edition

Printed in the United States of America

ISBN 978-0-61593-033-6

Slow Mountain Press
innisfree@pacific.net

For my wife, Kate

and

For my mother, Joan

Table of Contents

PART TWO

PART THREE

PART FOUR

v

Foreword

"Every poem is an anthology." I read that, or thought I read that, years ago, and the idea has echoed within me ever since. Going back to find it, though, the closest I've discovered is W.S. Merwin's line, "Every poem is a translation." It's a good one—thoughts, feelings and experiences don't come to us pre-verbalized—but it's different. My idea is more about the shoulders of giants we stand on, about the inspirations we get from the past and how they help to push us forward.

In organizing this book, which draws from ten years of writing done up in our forest home to the north-west of Willits, I've risked—in the notes at the end—what might look like highfalutin scholarship for the sake of making clear some of the influences that have found their way into my work. Consider it pulling back the curtain a little. Maybe I'm always a teacher. Maybe I want people to know more about poetry and some of my favorite poets. Maybe I'm just tired of people feeling like poetry is something they don't or can't understand. It's got a tradition, and reading it does require attention, but it's not as foreign a language as some stodgy old professors may have made it seem.

Po Chu-i, an eighth-century Chinese poet, supposedly read his poems to an illiterate servant woman, and if she didn't understand them, he went back and worked to simplify them even more. While I'm not sure every line of every one of these poems will make sense to every reader, or needs to, I do hope the grand bulk of them will.

Lastly, I want to mention the obvious: ten years is a long time. People change, times change. (If our moods vary as much as they do during the course of a day, how much more for a decade?) As a result, the styles of the poems here range pretty widely, as do the subjects and tones. I wander and meander and throw my voice; I yodel and howl and whisper by turns. If you don't like one poem, feel free to turn the page. Hopefully you'll find something there to like.

M.R.
Ukiah, CA
1-26-14

I

You ask why I stay in the green mountains:
I smile, and do not answer; my soul is at ease.

—Li Po

Earth's the right place for love:
I don't know where it's likely to go better.

—Robert Frost

This Morning's Prayer

Today, rather than suffused with light
or suffused with the grace of God,

suffuse me with fried potatoes and scrambled eggs,
suffuse me with a couple of good poems—
        read or written.

Today, suffuse me with a leisurely dog walk
and a hand to hold along the way.

A Story About a Man

The man there at the same table where
each morning coffee is served
and re-served, where a spoon
rings its way around the cup's rim
and where a quick swipe of sponge cleans the dribbles
that slide warm down the cup's side—Yes,
this man suddenly would like his morning paper
to say nothing of the battle dead, nothing
of the election of new leaders who will follow the old
in breaking even their most fundamental oaths,
nor does he want to see the scores of games or
ads for movies to preoccupy
or comics that can no longer make anyone laugh.

It's time, he decides, for a story about a man
like him, doing what he does as well as he can, a man
who suddenly has an insight, that life
is still worth it, that if you find
the right quiet mountain
there are still stars to watch slowly arc
across the night sky,
that such a mountain can be found,
and that before tomorrow morning stirs itself awake,
he will be the one to find it.

Follow the River

Follow from its ocean mouth
the river inland
up through mountains,
through gorges and twists,
through stony shallows, pools, forks,
upward,
then up further
to where rush becomes gurgle
and water sometimes flows below
forest loam,
where streamlets start
as morning mist beading,
trickling from leaves of madrone:

Here I have my home. Here I am
a student of beginnings and trajectory,
of saplings and dreams.

Redwoods

Reagan said
You seen one you've
Seen'em all

I say
You see one
Say Amen

See a second
Say it again

"You Come Too"

Look at this!
The sun is squinting finally through the gray,
& rain in the same instant is falling again, too.
Come & I'll show you where the little brook bursts
up from nothing,
just down there between the tanoaks
& huckleberry bushes.
I want to play Robert Frost & say,
"You come too,"
& show you where the deer trails poke through the
    undergrowth
& lead around the horseshoe of this ridge.
We'll grab redwood walking sticks
& jump off logs like little kids!
Why wait? This day's not gonna last forever
& the brook will dry up soon.
Come on! & we'll leave the world
to fight its wars.
Everyone else can find us when they're done.

To Simply Relax

I would give anything, she says,
For a little rest, a chance
To simply relax.

Sparrows chirp back and forth.
A woodchuck stands
On a mossy log to look around.
Far off in a patch of sun
A doe lies down and
Lets her eyelids grow lazy.

It is Sunday,
But the crickets
Would play their song
Whatever the day.

Getting the Swing

Learning again each autumn the ax swing,
The heft and focus, the ways of grain:

After the first weak swings I chide myself,
Then laugh in my gloves,
Assuring myself the learning's fun every time—
Till another awkward swing chips
Off the side &
                              out.

I take off my jacket, stand a moment beside Kate,
Ask about maybe breakfast.

Through the high oak branches
Morning sun warms my arms:

I'll get the swing again.

Like Golden Leaves

Golden leaves, auburn leaves
      leaving their trees
in October, in November,
      in December maybe—
they wait as long as they can,
      then loll and loop,
sway and spiral
      lackadaisically,
feeling no rush to join
      the earth just yet,
instead simply enjoying
      the wavering, tossed
as the wind tosses them
      until they do finally
touch down.
      Forgive me, Lady,
if I seem to hesitate.
      You are the soft ground
I am destined for.
      Let me look at you
from this distance
      another moment—
so welcoming,
      so inevitable,
so lovely
      I shall surely thrive
wherever I
      gently
land.

Third Day of Snow, Last Day of Vacation

Three days of snow and not a shoe print in it.
Only deer and now my dog.

My home is perched on the edge of this forest,
Hanging like a painting over the other world—

> *Stay in the trees,*
> *Keep to the forest!*

I walk a rough path to a small pool,
Stoop beside it, gurgle with it.

It says it would like more snow.
We'd both like to do the same thing tomorrow.

Stacking Wood

Stacking wood is not stacking wood,
it's stacking hours, days,
it's stacking silent moments
that a hand slips into place,
it's laying bricks the old fashioned way,
it's stacking generations of stacking,
the history of lives pulsing out,
it's learning the tradition,
the need to keep the hearth warm,
the home, the room where lives live out their days,
each in its own way.

Stacking wood is learning the art of placement,
of what belongs where,
of what will support what,
of guessing how long that support will need to last,
and of planning for the worst.

Stacking wood is losing yourself,
it's being wide-eyed dreaming,
it's pulling the soul back to its root,
reliving odd moments you'd forgotten to remember,
reliving them and finding more this time,
the subtle shades of light and phrase
the conscious mind can't quite catch.

Stacking wood is exhaustion
when you stop to notice it:
the arms burn, the hands ache,
and the spirit's been split from the body
as if by a swing of an axe

and flown off
to the corner of the yard you'd least expect,
and when the light's too slight to see by
you go and fetch it
and head inside feeling surprisingly alive
for the first time in months.

ii

The wood is a metaphor, of course,
just as the old man caught anything but a fish.
We stack ourselves, each other,
the books we've suffered through,
and the slow nights alone.
We stack photo albums of our grandfathers,
our wishes we'd known them better,
and we stack the stories we never got to hear.
And we stack our own stories.
They will burn hot and long through the winter.
They will see us through 'til spring.

The Name in the Forest

As the Stellar's jay sends its call down to me,
I send this poem to you, there where you sit,
There where you struggle with the blood
That rivers through you.
                              The forest
Knows your name: the ferns sigh it
In their shade, mushrooms burst from its loam,
And the broad Doug fir slowly chants it
In its lazy late morning sway.
                              The birds
Wink your name in Morse code all day long,
And when I shift my weight, the chair
Squeaks it like an excited child.
                              You,
You are the god of this forest, its creator,
Its redeemer: while you live, you keep it
Alive; when you die, you die so it might live.

My Savior Today

My savior today
Is a young local from way back,
From before any white man,
A Pomo of these mountains,
These streams he fished for salmon.
When around the fire at night
He told tales he'd heard in his wandering
Or came up with on long walks in the woods alone
Or during long nights beneath the gold-flaked stars,
Those dark faces listening around him bent forward,
Knew this was the sky talking,
The fire talking, the fish talking,
That it was the constant gurgle-speech of the rivers.

He died too young,
But those who knew him
Knew if they could live as he had—kind, giving,
Grinning whenever he could—
They'd be brought safely within the divine.

Your Jesus, my guy,
Ten thousand guys and gals
On each of ten thousand worlds,
They're all the same one.
Never mind the kind of fish.
Don't get caught up in the details.
They are all the same one.
Indeed, so too are you!

Portrait of the Buddha

The robe of the Buddha is flowing water.
   His head is a mossy stone.
His lap forms a swirling pool
   Where two fish become one.

His lids hang low like morning clouds
   Over eyes of brightest dawn.
He sits like a mountain where a tiger dwells;
   His prey and he are one.

Not a Damn Thing

Another sky gone gray
& not a damn thing done.

Nothing to be blamed for,
Nothing deserving praise.

I get up to add stove wood,
I sit to write a little poem.

Just that up & down,
Just that & just this.

Four Seasons Fast

i

deer antlers—
no match for spider webs
and nasturtiums

ii

summer dusk—
the flash of a bat
between us

iii

dog polishes
the abalone shell—
last night's rain

iv

winter ocean—
the momentary stillness
of a gull

Geraniums

"You may find yourself..."

Whose geraniums are these
Pinking up the corner of this deck,
Pinking a place in the gray-green dark redwood rainforest in
    a foggy autumn cool afternoon?

Whose geraniums?
Whose deck am I sitting on, under an eve, in a warm coat,
    relaxed, making myself at home?

Whose geraniums?
Whose hands dug the soil, planted and fertilized?
Whose domestic hands?
Whose spring hope?
Whose pink and smiling geraniums bounce in the gray-green
    foggy autumn redwood afternoon breeze?

Gathering

For Janet and Marissa

The sun goes down and dark ascends.
Wind whips up off coastal cliffs,
Swings through ravines and over high ridges.

Chimes ring on a home the woods hide
Where elves crawl from mossy stumps,
Silent but for the whisk of thick robes.

They gather and sit in an unknown grove,
Whisper and giggle over a kettle of tea
The moon brewed for the occasion.

Some nights my dog barks at them.
I call out a welcome, but there's no answer,
Just the breathing of a sly tribe in mist.

The Lesson of Fog

Driving home last night in fog,
high beams on, the light glaring back
in on me so the trees knew
who came through—
I wove corners up the mountain road
wondering about blindness, about
what crouches in the bleary periphery.

Now, as dawn stretches slowly
toward noon, the fog lounges in the woods
around the house—though maybe
this fog is my own grogginess,
the dirty windows, the glasses I put on
each day but don't often wipe clean, or
maybe it's this silent mood I'm in.

Maybe fog is water with an ancient lesson
to teach: that the silver mist
webbed between the dark & white
oak bark of this forest is
webbed between us all, that the crow
bouncing from branch to branch
is only the most obvious link.

Sideways Snow

The Little Chant I Wish I'd Had
for the Whole Long Mendocino Winter
of 2005-2006

Sideways snow
White-breath cold
Dusk coming on
Hope to hold

Dawn and a walk
Dog each day
Have to hunt her
Tracks both ways

Spring's been drowned
Rivers overrun
East in deserts
Only sun

Storm on the way
News again
Wet won't dry
Rain and then

Sideways snow
White-breath cold
Dusk coming on
Hope to hold

Faith in the Sun

The winter night has been so long,
has required so much stove wood
to keep this little house warm,
where you and I under our blankets
dream of a sun that has forgotten us,
a sun we still have faith in nonetheless.
We remember spring, planting seeds
that during three seasons lift
themselves and us with them
into the fresh air and toward
that ever-worshipped sun.
We do have faith still,
but it is hard, hard as the brittle ice outside
without even a pale moon
to shine down upon it.

What the Woodstove Gives

I fell the trees,
Buck the logs,
Split the rounds,
Then stack and later
Haul the wood inside,
Armful by armful,
To feed the fire
Over and over again,
And all it sometimes seems I get
Is ash
And more ash,
Ash way beyond what the garden can handle,
So then I have to haul the ash to the dump.

When will I open the woodstove
And find a sockeye salmon still thrashing,
Or a gift certificate to a fine restaurant,
Or a violin ornate with its cherry sheen?
How about a book of ancient Indian poetry I've never heard
        of and learn quickly to love,
Or a new set of snow chains that really do connect to my
        tires with a snap?
When will the stove deliver a pristine fossil of a saber-tooth
        tooth,
A simple head of lettuce,
Or a toad
That looks at me a minute with its aqua eyes and then hops
Into the nearest house plant?

None of these will happen anytime soon.
A little warmth is what we get from this life
Between times of cold.
And it is enough.

A little warmth and the ash of its making
Must be enough.

The Way of Water

On the Death of a Friend, January 4, 2008

It was the day the power was out
All day, the day my wife and I sat
In front of the woodstove heating
Water for tea, for oatmeal, for sponge baths,
The day we laughed at the shivering dog
When we let her back in the house,
The day I opened an old book
Of old blues and tried plucking notes
With too much twang, or not enough,
The day candles on the mantle turned
Our front room into a monastery,
The day we went to bed early and
Held each other for warmth and love.

But the real story of that day
Was outside, where water from the deluge
Of the night before broke out of
My shallow trenches, where mountain
Streams swelled and rushed, where
Water did as Lao Tzu knew, moving
At its own speed to the lowest place,
The lowest, largest, strongest
Destination of all: the unconquerable,
Utterly unfathomable ocean, there
To be perfectly what it always was.

II

this dewdrop world
is but a dewdrop world
and yet

—Issa

Is not love, with art, our only license to overreach the human condition, to be greater, more generous, more sorrowful if need be than is the common lot?

—Rainer Maria Rilke

The Starlings of Cloverdale

We make a dwelling in the evening air,
In which being there together is enough.
—Wallace Stevens

Pulled over on the side of the 101
To witness a late-November air show,
We stare up as starlings—
Thousands or tens of thousands—
Dive and twist and turn in unison
Through the blue-sky afternoon
Above a valley of golden vineyards,
Their every spiral and swoop unplanned
And perfect; and it hits me why
I follow you, and you follow me:
Our clumsy grace, the frantic ballet
Of our marriage and our love
Is beautiful; in the dash and
Cutback of our days, you and I, together,
Are beautiful, unpredictable, miraculous.

Tickling Her to Sleep

"Once I, Chuang Tzu, dreamed I was a butterfly and was happy
as a butterfly. I was conscious that I was quite pleased with myself,
but I did not know that I was Tzu. Suddenly I awoke, and there
was I, visibly Tzu. I do not know whether it was Tzu dreaming
that he was a butterfly or the butterfly dreaming that he was Tzu."

At this point not tickling her back
isn't even an option: her first brief moan
starts and I know where she's going,
or my hand, the one not holding
the book, ventures there without a mind
to make it or to feel any sacrifice
or even the contentment of philanthropy.
She commends my technique,
a subtle reward of years together,
the caresses so light they might be
from birds' wings or angels
curious to touch a mortal, the dearly
fallible. It's the way you might tickle
someone dying or just born,
someone arriving or departing
delicately, and as she slips to sleep
I wonder, in this case, which one it is.

Famished

I should feel the need to need
Food before I truly do,
By which I mean I should be
Mildly hungry before famished,
But I am not like you: my stomach
Doesn't work like yours, or
Is it my brain, the connection
Between the two? I'm satisfied
Until the sight of French fries
Sends me reeling, until the sound
Of bacon frying throws me
In spasms, until the scent of
A burger joint I'm passing
Makes its way through the vents
And I'm suddenly looking
At my wife's leg like the chicken
Hawk in the old cartoons sees
The barnyard chicken, on a rotisserie
Above a fire, sizzling, juicy. Her
Leg is so sweet and tender. Sometimes,
Suddenly, I've never eaten before.

Why You Should Get a Book on Dog Training Before You Get a Dog

I won't say who first allowed, even encouraged,
the dog to get up on the bed, with no concern
for time—night, past midnight, morning—
nor now with what might be going on, no attention
to whose legs or arms might be where, or where
whose hips are and what they're doing.

She's like a keen dancer, always finding the groove
between our bodies, where she wiggles
and shimmies us apart, the way a river divides
two mountains, or a new fence divides the world,
separating the happy haves from the unhappy have-nots.

The Broom

Only children, or
maybe only my niece, Sasha,
ask about the broom
hanging from the high rafter
in our living room,
the broom my wife and I
leapt over with a click
of our heels and landed
in marriage.

It was a slave ritual
we were told,
though later someone else
said the tradition came from
Ireland. A friend used it
to sweep up the floor of dust
and bits of bark from the huppah
we made of madrone branches
my best man and I pulled
from the forest.

The huppah
is a Jewish tradition, though
neither of us is Jewish.
The forest was just down the street
from where we live
with a broom
hanging in the living room
like a bouquet of dried flowers
thrown over a bride's shoulder
and caught, mid-air, upside-down,
by Time.

The Meaning of a Windy Day

The wind slips through branches of fir
And redwood, past madrone leaves
And oak leaves that whip themselves
Like minnows against the current.

Crows caw, chimes chime,
A mockingbird somewhere
Mimics some other bird, lovely.

The dog on the porch beside me
Works thumblessly on her bone,
And two hummingbirds,
Having finally discovered the feeder,
Fight a chattering duel for its juice.

All is green, active, gorgeous,
And none of it's ever meant more—
I have a baby niece asleep inside.
Sasha's asleep inside!

Thoughts on the Gift of a Green and Gold Checkerboard Blanket

For my Lita

We crochet with a yarn
that stretches back the generations
the art a series of improvements
each made half afraid
of insulting the past
the result's the blanket that keeps us warm
the stuff we cling to when the wind blows strong

these fingers have sprouted
from other hands
guided by the light of other suns
reached for a lover under other moons
when the stars were over a few degrees

these hands know the route
know the pattern
slip the hook through there
loop the yarn around
pull the hook back through the loop
tighten and repeat

each tribe each people each region

we are taught what we need to know
a way a design

to hold the ages together
a way to occupy the hands
a way to keep the body warm

Villain

For the folks at Magnetic Poetry
And for Ia

We caught her with a word in her mouth.
At nine months, she can choke on anything,
Especially something so small.
Her mother, Helen, got there first
And a finger-sweep found it:

Villain.

Was she speaking to the three of us
Sipping coffee and laughing at her fumbles,
At her awkward first steps and plops?

Was she giving us fair warning
Of things to come: valuables missing
And bodies found lifeless in shadows?

Or am I suddenly supposed to believe
A word is just a word,
Just a couple of meaningless syllables
Waiting to be pulled from our mouths?

The little blonde baby gave no hint,
Just smiled an innocent smile,
Turned and tottered away.

Armando

For Kate's Grandfather

Armando, old man,
oldest friend I've ever had,
how strange
is the strangeness of your absence.

What lack of imagination was it
made me think you would always be there
in the brown chair
with the back massager
and your slippered feet up on the stool?

You had your routine
at that old folks home—
each meal at the appointed hour,
the menu for the week up on the fridge
so you'd always know what to expect.

What did we expect?
That you'd go on forever?
That you'd always be there when we came,
when we left,
that you'd always answer when I said,
Hasta luego?

I say it again,
but, Armando,
where's your half of the banter?

A Life Lived So Well

Funerals make me nervous, not because of the dead
Body usually up front in a box, but
Because of what people are going to say
About what isn't in that box up front—
Kindly words about the living now that they're gone,
Words meant to tidy up a messy life, the kind of lives
Most of us have. So I was happy—well, not happy,
But...what? Not nervous?—to be sitting there
In the pew listening to the pastor and then the many,
Many friends of Mr. T, my Mr. T,
Jerry Todd, my best pal's father, a fine man
I'd had the pleasure of knowing nearly my whole life.
At a funeral like his you get to sit there
Without worrying what the next words will be
Because they can't be bad; he lived too well for that.
It's as if those good deeds done in life keep doing their
Magic, as if people like him, in their every decision
On how to live and how to be, were thinking ahead,
Not to some afterlife clowning around with a harp,
But to this life, my life, sitting in a pew
At 11 AM on a Saturday, listening
To speaker after speaker,
Not worrying about anything, laughing
When the stories were funny, wiping a tear
When a tear rolled down, celebrating
A good man, a life lived so well
No one has to stretch their tongue around a lie
To talk about him.

Grandmother's Shoes

Her old toes were bent to fit them.
The angle, the fine sharp angle
of her toes molded into those shoes—
sensible, conservative shoes
for a conservative, sensible woman.
Her little dollhouse miniatures business
became the business of her simple life:
the thin soup warmed again for dinner,
the warehouse space where she worked
and lived, the book of accounts that was
meticulous, literally double-checked—
down in English, back up in German.
Every figure, each flawless column
of such miniature numbers
told of the woman she was.
And how she giggled to recount
the story of the baffled tax man,
mid-audit, saying to her,
This must be wrong!
No one can live on so little...
No doubt when he said that
her toes were wedged into those
sensible, conservative shoes.

Guest Rooms

We all have guest rooms now,
        empty beds, empty dressers, shelves
of unread books, rooms

where dust returns far sooner
        and stays far longer than the family
in portraits on the walls,

like at Mom's house—
        pictures of me and my sister
in the sloppy collars of our youth,

in braces, in frames,
        behind glass to try to keep them
from fading any further.

We all have guest rooms now
        where we are all distant relatives
smiling at each other from years ago.

Finding Agate

For a favorite guest

Shey was up early, stretching
while water warmed
for morning tea.

She grinned, was eager
to get out to the rough coast
in winter storm.

Low-tide, she said,
would be just before noon—
about now actually—

and I can see her
in boots and raincoat,
reaching like she did at dawn,

finding agate
at every sandy step
of this outrageous life.

Emails to Tonya

After Hayden Carruth

i

When I found out, Tonya,
I was driving, then trying to calm
Kate and drive, then trying
To say goodbye and hang up
The cell phone and calm Kate and drive
Home, thank God, home.

ii

Watching the red November leaves
Beneath the maple outside my classroom,
How they blow in soft eddies,
Bumping each other, tumbling,
Resting awhile then tumbling again,
None knowing where any of them are
Going or why—Tonya, I realize,
With all my unanswered questions,
I'd be no better as a leaf.

iii

How do we do it, Tonya,
Teaching high school day after day,
Bringing them to "higher learning,"
As we call it, hoping they don't lose
Their innate sense of play?
You kept the balance, but how?
This is not a rhetorical question.

iv

"I am angry at no one
And I hope no one is angry at me."
So said a dying Holocaust girl
As told by her friend
In a film we watched today in class.
Angry at her?
I hope the dying don't always
Have such silly thoughts.
I guess I mean I hope you didn't, Tonya.

v

This job, Tonya, this profession,
takes too much time and energy
for which Kate and I are paid
more than we actually need right now,
so lately we've hired a cleaning lady
to buy back some of our time.
She's good and efficient, but she
has a penchant for rearranging things
ever so slightly. Now when
things are lost we need to stop
and think, "What'd she do with'em?"
Regrettably, this rule doesn't
work with lost friends.

vi

Yesterday, Tonya, was the department potluck
At Rosemary's house. Several people didn't show,
You among them. We knew you couldn't make it, though,
Because you sent out an email apologizing ahead of time,
Explaining that you'd be at your three year old nephew's
        birthday.

43

You included a couple of photos of your nieces and
        nephews
And said they were your best friends, but that's not why
You were missing. The food was good, and the company,
But there was no cake and no happy birthday.

        vii
One of our friends died
from bulimia, another
from obesity.
Tonya, the heart
can't handle extremes.

        viii
The other day, Tonya,
during silent reading
I thumbed through a book
of American poetry
and found this quote
from Emily: "Parting
is all we know of heaven,
And all we need of hell."
I wrote it on the white board
and asked the class what
they thought it meant. One
smart-ass said it meant
exactly what it said, but I
was having none of that.
Tonya, maybe he was right.
How do I know?

        ix
I haven't written many poems, Tonya,
In a couple of months, until now. What is it

About death that gets the mind moving?
All these MFA programs are senseless.
What would-be poets need is a departed friend.
How much should I charge for this insight?

     x
Denial is a river in
Africa. Tonya, I know you
Know this old joke. Why
Do we keep telling it
When no one laughs?
You kept us cracking up
And now I can't remember
A single line. Not one.
I keep thinking I don't need to.

     xi
The old haiku masters
left a final verse,
a last poetic statement.
I saw your students
weeping, Tonya, weeping.

"Love's Austere and Lonely Offices"

Up before dawn to gather
And take out the trash—last night
And the bear woulda gotten to it—

I make coffee, make a fire,
Cover the dog in her blankets, and then
Stop to listen to the silence.

There is none, even now.

The fridge hums, the fire crackles,
My own breathing seems to whistle a morning tune.

Kate's asleep.
A friend's asleep in the guestroom upstairs.

I remember an old poem,
One about a father up before everyone else and
Doing what needs to be done,
And I think of my father.
He's probably asleep, too,
Or sipping coffee alone.

The trash truck arrives.
I'm too awake to go back to bed.

The Feast and the Aftermath

Steve arrived from the coast with a cooler
He had to unpack for fear
It might go bad. He'd been there
For the weekend with a troop of fellow
"Bottom feeders," as we call them—
Those who still forage for their own food and
Who eat nearly anything—
but what a find it was:
Freshly smoked salmon, four kinds of wild
Mushrooms, the legal limit of three abalone
He was soon hammering tender out on the front step,
And a lovely Dungeness crab—
A culinary panoply fit for a king, let alone
A humble poet, who had only
To keep the dishes washed while Steve and Kate,
Both chefs of wide renown,
Kept the kitchen thriving with invention
And art—and even Kate,
Ever the vegan, broke down for the rich
Pink flesh of the salmon.
It was a gastronomical delight
Until it was a gaseous doom: Think
Of a septic tank boiling over black and rank;
Of the fetid stench of a ventless laundry room
At a booming diaper cleaning service;
Or of the inauspicious line-up of blue port-a-potties
Outside a Texan chili cook-off, each sweltering
With it own secret recipe of disgust.
I thought of none of that
That unholy afternoon when I went
To the bathroom to piss and farted
Something from the sulfur pits of Satan's darkest lair,
But I could not run for pissing still...

47

And still—good God, I could not breathe
Or hold the toxicity of my inhalation.
And I did not think—could not
Think, in fact—
That without putting a gun to our heads,
(Which for some reason I cannot condone)
We can never escape
Our sorry selves
When most we want to flee
From the tragedy of our repulsive
Humanity.

III

Ssh. Don't think.

—John Ashbery

When the cities lie at the monster's feet there are left the mountains.

—Robinson Jeffers

Listen

When Marilynn Manson,
America's loathed freak of rock,
was asked what he'd say, if he could,
to the two boys who shot up Columbine,
this is what he said he'd do—
and he didn't pause a second before saying it.

Listen.

Just after September 11th,
Thich Nhat Hanh,
world-renowned Buddhist monk and poet and teacher,
was asked by a New York audience member
what he'd say to Osama Bin Ladin
if given the chance.

Listen.

This is what he said he'd do, too.

Listen.

Desert Days

These are the desert days
These are the hot sun blister days
The days that scald
The days that scorch minds
Days that wobble in sun-fried eyes
These are the desert days
The cruel days
The dragging dead days
The days that hide behind rocks
Days that throw stones
Vicious days
Hateful days
Damnation days
These days are cracked
Dry, brittle days
Bleached bone days
Thirsty, ravenous days
Days that parch
These are the days that reoccur
That torment memory
Undefeatable days
Days that hang withered
Melting days
Days that seep from hands too tired to move
Days that banish
Days that punish
Days that laugh through the throats of lizards
Crawling days
Hissing, sidewinder days
Days that rattle in wind gusts
Dirty, sand-spitting days
Days that can't open their eyes
Blind, blinding days

Deaf, speechless days
Days that howl through a silence
Days that wait
Days that stalk
Deadly, fanged days
Days that eye horizons
Panting days
Unstoppable days
Vengeful days
Days that despise
Hungry, haunting days
Days that seek & find
Patient days
Days the sun returns for
Days the sun engulfs
Days the water seeks
These are the desert days
Desperate desert days
Dear God help us through them

Lorca's Body

Lorca's body is being exhumed.
Real attempts are finally being made
to find its whereabouts, to discover
which mass grave outside of which Spanish village
the great poet was taken to
and shot and tossed into
so many weeping years ago.

When it happens again,
when men come with guns
and pull people from homes for their thoughts,
their affiliations, for who they know
and for the words they speak,
I don't want to be left alive
to whisper of what I saw—
who they took and where,
which one was shot first, and
who put up the most resistance.
I don't want the breath that can speak of such atrocities
as an idle witness.

Bury me with them,
with the poets, the thinkers, the people
whose minds searched for truth
and whose tongues spoke it as well as they could.
I'd rather have both arms broken
because I refused to walk their line,
because I would not shut up.

I'd rather feel cold steel on the back of my head,
to hear nothing of the bullet blast
but the sound of skull shattering.
I'd rather have my last noise be the thud of my body

falling into the earth
beside others just as stubborn,
just as sure that the silence
of hands clasped over terrorized mouths
behind closed doors is a death
immeasurably beyond our own,
more painful, more irrevocable.

I'd rather stain the soil rich with my blood.
I'd prefer to unsheathe my bones slowly
While the years find shovels worthy of our unveiling.

I want to live well enough to be worth killing.

WestPoint

The old lie: Dulce et decorum est
Pro patria muri.
                    —Wilfred Owen

WestPoint has its literature professors, too,
Men and women who've read what the others have
And who have the kind eyes, or nearly
The kind eyes, of deep readers I've known.

How can they study what war has written—
Ideals blown like limbs, left like amputees—
And still continue to encourage such loyalty
When an army's true cause is to defend home so very rarely?

I know the battle of the classroom,
The young eyes in rows, alphabetical,
The way a teacher's words can spell truth, or misspell it.

Those eyes, those lives, deserve truth.

The Roads of Iraq

The roads of Iraq convulse, blasting
shrapnel across continents, across

years to pierce the dreams, the idle
bubbles in the mouth of a young boy

who stares out a summer window at birds,
wondering, if he grabbed his toy gun

and canteen and began walking now,
how far he could get down that road

before his family found out
he was gone.

Teaching War Theory

I half want to say
nothing, to stand before them

in a silence thick
as smoke from a blasted village;

instead I speak
like a distant ship lobbing bombs

into a desert,
while lizards in their ears sleep.

Turning Off the Engine

Turning off the engine,
pulling on the e-brake:

such minor movements
shouldn't count for so much.

We push open our doors,
swing our feet out and

place them on the land
outside our house, where moss

crawls the pace of years
up trunks that don't mind,

and orange madrone glows
like sunset during the day's

last hour. This is the hour
we pass on the right

to witness from home, hoping
the afternoon breeze can blow

from us the well-earned exhaustion
that throws us to the couch

and through which we hear
news of troops and "casualties,"

major doings of the world
that, if we had not sold

our precious minds and time,
would horrify us even more.

In Any Parking Lot

Eating fast food
in a parking lot
between Home Depot, Staples
& a Lazy-Boy showroom,
in any town, or every town—
our town today—
belly to the steering wheel
of an old Mustang
with a smashed front bumper
and a rusty, paint-peeled roof,
a woman sat
alone with her jowls,
her hand digging in a paper bag,
her working mouth red as catsup spurting
or Ronald McDonald's grin
or the bars that cross
the American flag
waving like a friendly child
above us.
And what was I doing there?
I was caught like she was,
like you are,
on the hungrier side of those bars,
needy, desperate,
in the land of plenty
but never-quite-enough,
rushing with another shopping list,
insatiable, American.

Ode to the Letter "L"

You used to be
one face on the blocks I stacked and toppled,
one day of Sesame Street,
the letter on Laverne's polyester shirt
that was groped, famously, by everyone.
You were what we sang
when we sang
with no particular song in mind—
                La-la la-la la
You were a warm sound.
You began words—
                Life, Love, Lily, Laughter—
bright things, reasons to live.

Now, more than anything,
I think of kids putting
thumb and forefinger to their heads
to call each other "Loser,"
or the shape of mini-malls
plaguing America with their non-descriptness.
You have become for me
an end sound—
                Final, Dull, Pastel.

The Only Mammal

The only mammal on earth
more abundant than man
is the rat—

Cartoon women leap helplessly onto chairs,
yelping and lifting their skirts to show a little leg;

Trucks disguised as rats
sneak toward houses with vats of poison,
making America safe;

Winston Smith,
with his face attached to a rat cage,
screamed until his soul slid out,
leaving his eyes hollow as bubbles
Big Brother eventually popped;

In England, dogs were bred to kill them—
one Manchester terrier got 117
in under 60 seconds;

And who knows how many we got
just by dropping a couple of bombs on Japan
free of charge.

The rat's worst enemy is man—
something they have in common with man.

Since It's Only a Matter of Time

When bombs lambaste my homeland
    To rid it of a tyrant,
When artillery shells rain down
    Like apocalypse stars—

Rather than depleted uranium,
    Please, give me roses and geraniums;
Instead of white phosphorus,
    Bathe me in daffodils and lettuce.

Forgetting the World

Even here, resting beside a little rush
Of river feeding Lake Kennedy on Vancouver Island
Upon whose smooth rocks tourists snap photos
Every day of spring and summer,
A place you can call the most beautiful swim spot
On earth and speak with some confidence,

Even here, it is so hard to do,
To forget the world we rode so far to leave behind.

I turn to the motorcycle on the highway's shoulder,
Making sure it's still there,
And I worry about finding the Comax ferry in time,
And I think of home, the return to school, work,
The bills piling in our absence,

And I remember Han Shan,
Some thirteen hundred years ago,
Who got away, and stayed away,
By walking up a mountain.

And I then remember that even he
In some of those poems
Had to admit
Even he
Couldn't completely forget the world.

As Simple as This

At a campground near sundown
on the Olympic Peninsula in Washington State,

with the smell of smoke
from family fires mixing with
fir & fern & blackberry—

on an evening as simple as this—

I heard a little girl
raise her voice to a joyous shriek,

    Hello Grandma!

And I thought:

Maybe there is hope.

For this sad, suffering, sweet, green world,
maybe there is hope.

Water

We are not so different, you and I.

I am still.
I am wild.
I rage and tickle by turns.

I am within you, that you may live,
Yet when you are within me, beware.

You will find I am lowly.
You will find I fall, as if in love, gently,
Or, like lost love, in a torrent.

Cut me, I am not hurt.
Divide me, I do not care.

Even you who fear me can put me together again.

You can swallow me.
I can swallow you.
That's fair, isn't it?

Do not call me unfriendly.
Wave to me,
I might wave back.

IV

In a culture that likes to think it is founded on the powers of logical, rational mind, the term "imaginary" has taken overtones of the trivial or the frivolous.

–Jane Hirshfield

Tell all the truth, but tell it slant.

–Emily Dickinson

Five Tanka on the Journey to Japan I Have Yet to Take

After sitting
fourteen hours—
Japanese asphalt
feels ancient,
rigid beyond compare

*

A land where
everyone exults
in their slippers—
my favorite pair forgotten
half a world away

*

Mid-city bustle
of taxis motorcycles mini-vans
and exhaust—
but here they have such
black hair

*

The Tsubo stone
where Bashō
was moved to tears—
I have only
mild allergies

*

Cricket chirps
last longer than this—
packing a suitcase
is too soon
memories of Japan

Dear Reader

Some mornings you
are more than just
an imaginary reader.

You become a sultry
imaginary lover: my
words caressing you,

you carelessly insulting
them, they—ever
insecure—strangling you.

It is a tale of beauty
and horror, of dark words
stealing away after

wiping clean their prints
and arranging your lovely
auburn hair just so.

An Idiot's Guide to Morning

The sound you hear is not angels humming,
Or an atomic blast,
Or a beetle loose in the room.
It is an alarm.
The difference is great.

The two things you stand on, feet,
Slip into the slippers you should find nearby.
They are called slippers
Because feet slip into them.
Not all things are so well named.

Go to the bathroom by sitting or standing,
Whichever feels easier
And makes less of a mess.

Eventually take off whatever you're wearing and step
Into the shower. Scrub your body with soap.
Generally, the places hardest to reach
Need the most attention.

If the towel stinks, it may be old, well used,
In need of laundering.
The room may have mildew.
Then the stench is general
And the towel may be fine. For now.

Get dressed according to the fashions of the day.
Good luck interpreting the fashions of the day.

Have a way you like your coffee
And stick to it.
This will tell people something about you:

You like your coffee black
Or with cream.
Sugar is significant.

If you read the newspaper,
Don't believe what you read.
Read a couple of comics to keep from being dull.

Breakfast is the most important meal of the day.
Say, "Sourdough," when asked about toast.
Say, "Over medium," when asked about eggs.

And always, always say,
"Thank you."

Dental Work

I. Patient Questionnaire

What do you consider to be the most important factor in making sure that your dental experience is a positive one?

I hear your chairs are comfortable,
Laid back, cushioned, but also
That you sometimes use tools designed to harm
Rather than help the mouth develop
Its own unique personality: my mouth,
You know, has a lot to say and doesn't
Need to be twisted into submission;
Therefore, simply sweet talking my teeth
Into the straight line of whiteness
Is preferred, and an apple fritter with my coffee.

What are your goals and desires regarding your dental experience?

I'd like to leave with super teeth,
Bionic teeth, teeth that make others tremble,
Teeth I could take out, or that
Could come out on their own, but
Only when I wanted of course, like
I could be standing there in line at the DMV
And when I heard someone being rude,
A customer or the tired, bitchy worker lady behind the desk,
I could just grimace a bit then spit a few teeth
Like spitting bullets only they won't quite kill,
But maybe lightly maim,
Enough to leave welts, a few open wounds, enough
To let them know that maybe it's time to shut the hell up;
And then, rather than fall to the ground,

My teeth would spin back my way,
Like little glossy boomerang teeth
Back to my half empty grin
And slide up into my gums,
Tight like they never left me.
Then, as the other folks in line applauded,
I might bow slightly.

What do you like most about your smile?

Frankly, I'm proud that my smile's still there,
That it hasn't fallen off and been lost over the years,
Because it has come close:
There have been tough times,
Ragged, frantic times
When my smile's been misplaced, missing;
Other times I've had to put it in my pocket,
Tuck it down there deep,
Or lock it away in a box
Like tarnished heirloom jewelry,
But there was always something,
Sunshine, some dumb sit-com or a silly dance to remind me:
Remember your smile,
Remember your old child smile!

What do you like least about your smile?

I wish my smile were a little bigger
And inflatable like a blimp so I could fly;
I'd like my smile longer and thin
So kids could jump rope with it
And I could lasso wild broncs from across whole prairies;
I'd like a smile deep enough for fish to swim in
Or philosophers to debate about;
I'd like two apples for a smile,
Though I don't know if I'd let ponies munch on them.

If you could have the perfect smile, what would you desire?

I'd want my smile to stop traffic,
Stop women mid-step, stop air pollution
And global warming, stop cancer in all its forms
And every other kind of disease. I'd want a smile
That could put an end to war and greed
And all human need,
A smile that could stop injustice,
Idiocy, ignorance, bad breath
And grocery stores from charging so much,
A smile that could end all the sloppy tendencies of humanity.
Then, when the world is made anew by my fine smile,
I'd like to stop stop signs from being so consistently dull,
Because it's time for us make some progress!

II. Novocain

While my dentist lives out dreams
of being an ancient Roman sculptor,

and I become a timeless David
with my beauty nearly restored,

the hygienist, aiming her funnel like a wand,
sucks rose petals from my mouth,

and I fear, oh, I fear she will think
my marble heart has warmed to love.

III. It Is Not a Dentist's Chair

It is not a dentist's chair
but an ear-popping rocket take-off,
a brothel lounge couch,
a sterile death bed and I see the light—
I'm being beckoned toward the light!
It's a sunny picnic-in-the-park day,
a whale's eye floating over me,
a crystal ball glowing,
a left-fielder blinded by a pop fly at noon.
It's a leather interior seat leaned back for love,
a Disneyland ride I had to wait too long for,
a gurney in a chopper over Viet Nam.
It's a lighted stage for my soliloquy,
a gas lamp at midnight,
a TV watched for too many hours
without ever blinking.
It's a concussion,
a blackout,
a flashlight, an Armageddon,
an interrogation trained and funded by the CIA,
but I will not tell them!
I will not tell them it is a dentist's chair.

An Art Museum That Might Get Built

Scale your life down, like an architect's scale model
Of an art museum that might get built.
Cars in that driveway never bend fenders,
Those breezeless bushes never need trimming,
And the human figures—mid-stride,
Facing toward or away from the cardboard doors—
They lack any confusion,

Unless in the back of their plastic heads
They worry a competing firm will win the design
And leave them glued where they stand
In front of a building that will not exist,
Unable ever to see the exhibition inside, or
Unable ever to drive home maybe changed by art.

Self-Portrait by Vincent Van Gogh

i

What sees more clearly than a painted eye
unburdened by mind or history,
infallible as only fiction can be?

Vincent, you with heart enough
to try to spread with a pistol blast
over a field of wheat,

your eye now never wavers in any sunlight
but holds me framed
in this cold stare.

I look at you and lose my purpose.
I turn away and you follow.
I forget you only to remember you still

so silently there—a jury, a god,
an incarnation in paint as thick
and haphazard as blood,

your face as resolute as time,
as true as death,
and every bit as immortal.

ii

What but these bold black splotches
can form eyes so steady
their inquisition feels final?

In them, I, too, become a painted falsehood
with the heavy brush of judgment
my creator, my tormentor:

my face, a new system of slashes,
of colors joining and overriding each other,
raging in every direction;

my nose, too, a mangled blur;
my ear, too, a vague shape;
my beard, as well, a fire in a dark night.

The Mona Lisa Is a Clock

The Mona Lisa is a clock
Advertised full-bleed on a magazine page
I taped beside the classroom clock
High up, center, on the eastern wall.

Always her strange smirk
That, just now, even in this deformed
Sepia rendition, pulls me into it:
Dark, colorless, cavernous.

I put on my headlamp, slip inside
Those lips and, there among the stalactites
And clock-work gears,
A back-bent man in overalls

Welcomes me, hands me
A pair of dirty gloves and a huge wrench.
He says it's good to have,
But that he hopes I won't have to use it.

On the cave wall behind me
Light pours in through the slit I climbed through.
It's the shape of a cat's eye.
The gears shift with the heaviness of a minute.

The man in overalls is gone.
I am wearing his overalls.
From the shadows a cat comes out,
Rubs on my pant leg.

I somehow know the gears of time
Will not need me to use the wrench.
I sit and wait
For someone who will come to replace me.

The Wireman

Suppose the wireman I made
Years ago were to come alive

And dive like a slinky
Off the mantle to stand

All of one foot tall
On the table before me—

Poor fool, he'd no doubt soon relate
His yearning for a wire mate.

Two Thinkers, Bookends

Rodin's masterwork was mass-produced
by a major chain bookstore, purchased
by my mother, and given to me
in a box wrapped with gold ribbon.

I set them on either end of a stack of books
where they looked like brothers sulking
on two sides of a room, lashing at one another
like dogs with the teeth of their thoughts
for faults they both share—grumpiness,
indecision, lethargy. Each refused to relent.

To separate them I took one to school
and placed him on a shelf where I sometimes
use him to illustrate a word or concept:
conundrum, ponder, meditate.
Then I put him back, leaving him in peace
to ponder the woes of modern education,
a meditation for which there is little reward
except a dust of dry human skin.

The other has remained at home, here
beside my desk, crammed between Whitman's
Leaves of Grass and a King James *Bible*,
hunched over like he's sick from trying to decide
between body and soul, between prayer
and poetry.
            Once I saw him lift his head finally,
stare up at the ceiling and a little to the left,
perhaps coming to the conclusion that
talking to God and crafting a true poem
might somehow be two aspects of the same
glorious consciousness, but

just as his lips parted to finally speak
he returned his rock head heavily to his stone fist.

At the Symphony

Behind the fluttering butterflies of her eyelids
Her exhausted mind leaned toward sleep
And learned again the magic of music,
How it tosses away the sandbags in the way
Of her normal clumsy waking mind
And then lets that mind grow long regal legs
And wings until it soars, a Pegasus,
Over the square buildings with so many locked doors
And all those cars angling to get ahead of each other,
Until she flew in blue sky, with the few clouds
And, in the distance, mountains—and surely one
Somewhere nearby was Olympus.

Each note was her nectar, every tone her ambrosia.

She dined with the gods in that immortal hall
That lay hidden in the miracle of her skull
Where pictures began to flash with each trumpet blast,
With each blow of the oboe and crash of the symbols:

Crowds crossing a downtown intersection,
A honeybee landing and disappearing into a hexagon,
An anti-aircraft missile shooting toward the heavens,
A first autumn oak leaf falling to her redwood deck
Just beside her hand and a glass of lemonade.

And then, as the swell of violins became a hapless wailing
Of babies in an orphanage, she saw
That the conductor in his tuxedo waved his arms
In those sharp commandments for her,
That her very synapses were the lightning strings touched
To enrich the suffering world with all this blessèd sound.

She was the flute, and the bassoon, and the trombone,
And every delicate nuance of this timeless creation,
And for a moment, for a movement, for a night,
In the twilight of her consciousness,
She believed, unquestionably, in God.

Light Through Windows

Admiring strands
Of afternoon sunlight
Coming through the kitchen window,
She missed her sister,
Missed braiding her famous blonde hair.

Why were there flowers on the curtains?
And why curtains at all when she never closed them?
What had her sister said on the subject?

Memories themselves, she decided,
Are like looking through lace
Into a locked house where you once lived
With your sister,
Brushing her hair, braiding her hair
To near perfection.

The Curtains

By night they change the color of the curtains.
   —Jerzy Jarniewicz

The curtains are iguanas hanging,
changing color to suit
their moods. Well, what of my mine?

I've been watching these lizards since dawn.
I don't dare look away. They will lunge
and eat me like fallen fruit.

That one, I swear, I saw years ago
on a dirt road in Costa Rica.
I stood stock still in village mud

until it scampered back into the bush.
It doubled-back to here.
It's been disguised until now.

Murmurs

When the murmur only he heard
became a roar, our hero stood with a start,
and from each pew, eyes
of every human hue turned to stare.

You have been this man, and you
have been the Roman soldier
in each of those judging eyes.

*

By the time Time
caught up with our hero, all
his grand pronouncements
(each one a revelation)
had wilted to mere murmurs.

The sun of heaven had darkened
his skin, even the foot
that wore a sock.

*

The street held him like its bird,
like a pigeon murmuring,
and then he flew
away.

Toward a Theology for Starfish

Would the starfish be wrong
To suppose itself made
In the image of the orange blur
Warming the tide pool at noon?

What rite, what sacrifice
Would such a god require?
Should the starfish fast?
    For how long?
Should it go on a pilgrimage?
    Where to?
Could it possibly bow down
Any lower than it already is?

If it were to pray,
What would a pious starfish say?

And if it did give prayer a try,
How long should it wait for its god's reply?

Lines Written Just Before Nothing Occurred

May 21, 2011

A few hours from now will begin the end times.
But is your soul saved? Are you ready to leave?
O why have you scoffed at these warnings of mine?

The Lord gave us prophets, His heavenly signs,
And haven't I begged you, "Believe, please, believe
It will not be long until the end times"?

I won't ever see them, but tomorrow's headlines
Will confirm that the skeptic in you was deceived
In scoffing at all of these warnings of mine.

For this dark world has strayed so far from divine,
And the wrong once made by our ancestor Eve
A few hours from now will beget the end times.

Then the last shall be first—it's the Lord's grand design—
And the first shall discover it's too late to plead.
Woe unto the scoffers of warnings of mine!

With both sorrow and glee, I pause for this rhyme,
Sorrow at knowing you'll have so much to grieve,
Yet what fortune to witness the promised end times!
Ah, but you scoffed at these warnings of mine...

A Humble Prophesy

In the brilliant curvature of its shell
The chick might well guess that all creation
Is packed there with him, & for him, until
His restless beak pecks out to revelation.

So, too, our night sky was shattered open
By Galileos who through telescopes
Could see nearly to eternity. Then
Began the questions: strange fears, stranger hopes.

Once, camping, I dreamed of leaves in my hair
& woke to find an ant—no, a few—no,
Thousands beneath me, on me—everywhere!
Well, what's life if not a startling show?

Now, this year, friends, that show will vastly expand:
We'll find alien life, single-celled & monumentally grand!

Fashionably Late

You'll be late to your own funeral,
my mother has often warned me,

& I hope I am! Imagine it: the classical music
eventually ending in a quiet chapel,

mourners in pews looking down
at their watches, fidgeting with hems,

glancing over their shoulders again
at the double doors that don't creak open,

while up front the minister in his stiff chair
shakes his head and sends off an exasperated prayer.

Slave

An old slave doesn't have much
living, and even less dying
on his same old cot
of straw and memories,

but he does have that glorious day
he and Millie got married
just outside the shack here.

When they jumped that broom
he thought they'd fly so far to heaven

they'd never have to land.

My *Nine Horses*

i

Glancing down at my *Nine Horses*,
It hits me suddenly that my nine
Really make it eighteen, and that

If nearly every poetry reader in America
Has a copy—and there must be a couple
Of dozen—nine is entirely

Untrue. And, Mr. Collins, you may not
Know me, but I assure you, I am not
Someone who likes to be lied to.

ii

Glancing down at my *Nine Horses*
Where it sits beside my coffee mug
On the well-named coffee table, I wonder

Suddenly if you too have a copy lying
Around, allowing those nine horses
To see themselves and how silly they look

Harnessed to a wall that has yet
To click its tongue, as good riders do,
A wall still deciding which way to go.

iii

If I had nine horses I wouldn't
Nail them to a wall like a makeshift
Cross—I'd give them to charity:

Some homeless shelter or orphanage
Where children could go to sleep
Each night dreaming of sugarplums

And horses waiting in the stable for them
To leap upon, to ride until they find
A sunset to gallop straight into.

iv

Nine was always the easiest number
When it came to multiplication, the trick
My third grade teacher taught me—

Bless her soul, and I don't say that often—
The way the 5 and 4 of 54
Together equaled nine, a symmetry

Only nature, the maker of shells,
Could create. When we get busy creating
It ends up as sad as those nine horses.

v

If you had to be a beast, one you
Aren't already, a wild horse out on a prairie
Wouldn't be a bad choice:

Running under a sky that darkened
And lightened in a cycle as mysterious
As horse birth, unless you lived the misery

Of leaving behind one of the herd, a mare
Or an old stallion with a busted knee,
There to wait for evening and the wolves.

vi

Glancing, again, down at that book,
The *Nine Horses* I still haven't finished
Reading, trying not to get too caught up

In the journeys of daydreams they take and
Getting caught instead in my own, I wonder
About the horse or horses those squares

Were modeled from: the field they stand in,
The wooden trough of water they drink from,
The hawk flying silently by.

vii

Ride a horse and you are a cowboy,
Which makes about as much sense
As anything these days: news that isn't

News, wars that aren't ours
To be fighting, a fine democratic nation
Too punch-drunk from late night

Movies to know when to vote or why—
A people content to chew on any alfalfa
Anyone throws in our corral.

viii

Art about art about art
Can't be too promising: this poem
Can't pay you back next Tuesday

Regardless of what it tells you, can't say
It won't make a pass at your wife
When you leave to go to the bathroom

Or to fix another drink. This poem
Is thankful you invited it, though, for sharing
Your lovely home. Dinner was excellent.

ix

Glancing yet again, I notice those nine horses
Are still panting after the long run between us.
Mr. Collins, I'd like to ask you

To raise a glass of your ever-present wine
And toast these hard-working steeds
Who won't know the joy of young riders,

Nine fine animals stuck up there, nailed
Like old family portraits, silent as tickless clocks,
Caged like nine songless cockatiels.

The Ballad of Black Bart and the Irish Lass

Now, I'm no scholar or historian nor a cloak & dagger sleuth.
I don't let cold hard facts intrude on softer, warmer truth.
Don't ask where or what he robbed or how many men he
    killed.
A legend is a rare thing & requires more than facts to build.

Yes, Black Bart was a scoundrel & a horse thief & a
    bottom-drawing snake,
A rapscallion son of a bitch & an outlaw bastard rake.
He'd agree to all of these but say, "A poet, too, I am.
You can call me what you like & you can catch me if you can."

Meanwhile, Lady Sarah was a red-haired lass from far-off
    Galway Bay,
& men there went into mournin' the day her beauty sailed
    away.
In the new world she was welcomed by everyone she met.
They were charmed by her graces & her heavenly accent.

Oh, she had a tender disposition, & her smile made strangers
    friends.
Each city opened wide its doors, & proposals soon began.
But ever-eager seeking new sights & adventure she went west,
Which is where she met foul Black Bart, a gold locket on her
    chest.

Well, that stagecoach driver sat tremblin', his hands high up
    in the air,
& Black Bart said chucklin', "Friend, you can jump on down
    from there."
& then he called for the folks in the carriage to come out one
    by one.

That's when Lady Sarah stepped magnificent into the
	California sun.

Now, Black Bart, you can be sure, was never one for lack
	of words.
He was a poet first, yet he was now struck dumb by the
	vision of this girl.
Turns out hers was a salty tongue, & she was as brash as
	she was fair—
Good God, she gave him hell! You shoulda heard that
	woman swear!

But he drank her abuse like it was whiskey from a divine
	mountain stream
Till he was dizzy drunk like he'd never been & halfway
	stayed it seems.
For what else can explain the change that overtook him
	then?
It was like he found religion & had turned away from sin.

She demanded that he let her go, & that's exactly what
	he did—
First time he'd done what he was told since he was a
	knee-high no good kid.
& as he watched that wagon leave, spinning dust into
	summer air,
He wondered if she'd miss her locket & shook his head
	because he cared.

'Fact, from heart to parchment after that, friend, poems
	poured & poured.
Verses came as if God-given—but 'course he didn't believe in
	the Lord.
He hadn't believed in much at all, but now he believed in
	love,
Figured for eternity it'd fare better than anything up above.

101

Well, days went by & frigid nights & his was a lonely life,
& he thought of stopping his wily ways & settlin' with a wife.
Yet for wife he knew there was only one, like the moon alone
      is grand,
& he pulled out that locket again just to hold it in his hand.

You might not believe if I said he wept, so, friend, I won't.
If you think real men never cry, then keep thinkin' that they
      don't,
But as fall fell into winter & his fires fought frost at dawn,
Ol' Black Bart kept on thinkin' of her & of love & where
      she'd gone.

Then late one night by campfire light he was so lost in
      thoughts of her
He didn't hear footsteps till they were near, but he was quick
      to draw & turn,
& he fired so fast both the move & the blast came as a shock
      to him & the boy—
No, not a deputy or bandit but a child, not a rifle but a
      wooden toy.

No one ever saw that devil Black Bart around these parts ever
      again.
He vanished like that frost at dawn, but legends don't so easily
      end.
He wound up searchin' for her down in San Francisco Bay,
& folks there knew of his red-headed love, but where she went
      they couldn't say.

Some stories have it he went to the Yukon where rivers with
      gold do flow,
Others that he sailed for China or rode south to Mexico.
I'll tell you this, wherever he is he's got that locket in his hand,
& he's dreamin' of a lass, a fiery lass, with the grace of
      Ireland.

Now, if you're accustomed to hearin' a moral at the end of
          a tale told,
You're gonna have to supply it yourself—I'm not so wise or
          not so bold.
The ways of this world are a mystery, friend, 'specially
          concernin' the ways of the heart,
& the ways of the heart concern everyone, even an outlaw
          like ol' Black Bart.

V

Poetry... I, too, dislike it.

−Marianne Moore

Artists report on the inner life, and the inner life distinguishes us from centipedes, although I may underestimate centipedes.

− Jane Kenyon

First Thought

For Jim Lyle

A fox stops in the sun
between distant trees.

With a gun, I wonder,
could I hit it?

You see, John Wayne got to me
before poetry.

My Prelude

For Colleen

She led me down aisles
of dust & musty shelves,
of sneezes & sighs, of questions
& wise bindings,

& stopping she scanned
& grabbed a volume
thin as a frail friend's hand
& opened & read,
& her breaths inexorably led to

> *A lonely cab-horse steams and stamps.*
> *And then the lighting of the lamps.*

& I heard that horse.
My eyes were those lamps,

& I've strolled those cobbled streets ever since.

Poem Beginning with My Imperfect Beard

Some mornings I put my beard on sideways
And don't notice 'til I return home in the evening.

Suddenly all the day's laughter,
Much of which I joined, makes a new kind of sense.

You without a strand of hair out of place—
    Or missing altogether—
This poem is not for you.

You get hair spray, fancy shampoos, mousse.
Poetry is reserved for the rest of us.

The Morning Poets Meet

The table would need to be long
For all of us to sit together,
To share our solitude together,
And the thousands of chairs lined up
Side by side, every different sort,
From the stiff backed, the velvet,
To my wicker folding chair.
William Stafford, I would have you
Sit first, and who would sit
Beside you, Gerald Stern, Naomi
Shihab Nye, so many brilliant minds,
So fresh in the early hours.
The window would need to be wide
Too, from the prairies of Kansas
To Calcutta's cityscape, the rain
Of Kiev to San Antonio's parched
Mountains, when above every scene
The eastern sun rose into an endless
Metaphor of color and rebirth.
And all those hands would reach
To write, using everything from
Quills to laptops, while cups of
Coffee and tea steamed waiting
For the stream of inspiration to
Subside just long enough for each
Poet to stop and sip, and if they
Glanced down to where I sat,
They wouldn't need to know my
Name, it would be enough to see
Just another eager poet of the dawn
Just about to finish another morning poem.

Water's Edge

Is this poem you
throwing yourself
up and out of your
element, arching,
an eye on me
before splashing
back like a trout, or

have you leaned
yourself down,
thrust your wide-eyes
into my world
to see where I
live among river
rocks and crawdads?

No matter. One
of us is mostly
wet, and the other
mostly dry. You
choose: gills or
lungs? We're all
breathing somehow.

Famous

He tired of fame before the fame was won.
     —Ezra Pound

Let's all get famous &
get on MTV melodiously
or on ESPN with the heavy weight
slam & show the world
that poetry's not just the
dense word clusters in
musty books professors are
prepared to test us on.

Let's all get famous,
let's get laughed at on Letterman
for thinking syllables
can outlast eternity
& when the poems end
the studio air will have still
the slack-jaw schwa
of incomprehension & awe.

Let's all get famous &
cover magazines with our
lust-pout lips & lyric eyes
that gems might be tossed into
for luck & relief
from the tedium of the
Armageddon long line
of the grocery store.

Let's all get famous & drive
bright cars down dark
Italian lanes to our friend's

chateau for a weekend
between pyramids & a moon
we wept into being
to fan our soft love's
warm brow with while singing.

Let's all get famous like
the redwoods & grow beyond
the scope of mammal eyes
& green needle tips will be
our tongues & creek water
our blood & our laughter
autumn wind swirling to the stars
& for them & to become them.

Let's all get famous & wield
that fame & cling to it
until we find ourselves like
gray-haired long-haired rockers
performing in old bowling alleys,
straining our throats to drown
the sound of strikes that
are not & won't be ours again.

What the hell? Let's all
just go & get some drinks
& write each other silly poems
on napkins—forget fame
& call it a day.

My Library

The poor librarian begins to stamp her feet
and weep.
       —Mark Strand

I own a lot of books. My wife
would say, *Too many*, would say,
Give them away, trade them in
or burn them—whatever works
to rid the house of clutter and dust.

Of course, you would say, *Why*
are you telling me this? Discuss it
with your wife, find the compromise,
that you don't have the time
to listen to my marital squabbles.

But you, Mark Strand, there
with your smug smile on the back
cover of your *Selected Poems*, you
have nothing but time: you and
your teeth aren't going anywhere.

So let me continue: I have a lot
of books, and yours is one I turn to
every couple of years, enough that,
if there ever were a fire, I would
spare your volume from it,

or I would try to pull it from
those quick flames, assuming I had
already saved my own dubious verse,
and that my wife, in her fury,
hadn't tied me tightly to a wooden chair.

Kerouac's *Book of Haikus*

O, I've been there, brother, & made it back by thumb
    Soul weary & frozen but never fully numb
I've stood on the cliff-top staring at the crashing blue
    Thinking of Kerouac's *Book of Haikus*

In the deserts between us sturdy flowers bloom
    Bright as the blaze in a hermit's orange room
You can keep *On the Road* & *Mexico City Blues*
    Friend, I've got Kerouac's *Book of Haikus*

Mountains & mountains rove ever undone
    While rivers between them dance with the sun
Keep your *Desolation Angels* & *Big Sur*, too
    Me, I've got Kerouac's *Book of Haikus*

Yes, I was gone a good while, on a round trip by thumb
    Backpacked as Japhy or any Dharma bum
But breathing deep as the forest, fresh-eyed as dew
    For me, friend, it's Kerouac's *Book of Haikus*

Bixby Canyon

Everyone feels something there, I'm sure,
Would have to, there
Over that vast bridge with its impossible reach
From one side of the canyon
Clear over to the other,
A feat which would be a hike in your best boots,
With the wind and gulls wheeling
Above you and those high cliffs of Big Sur, California.
Everyone feels something there, I'm sure,
Especially zipping quick around those curves—
You don't need a Porsche or Ninja
To get to leaning into each twist,
Hooting like you should when you're thrilled to be alive
And when you're pushing that life
A little farther than is maybe safest.
Everyone feels it—they must—
Whether or not they know about that old cabin down there,
Ferlinghetti's cabin,
Where he's spent so much time,
And all his friends,
Even Kerouac, who strode down to the sea
And learned to translate it, transform it,
Transmorph it into its elemental sounds—
The slooshing stretch of vowels,
The crash of consonants on granite,
The rhythms that have been rolling there
Since before any time we can ever imagine
And are still there, singing—
Angel splash, ebb and flow!
Everyone feels something there, I'm sure.
Everyone feels something there, I know.

Mugwort

Snyder said to "Learn the flowers,"
and like most advice I've received,
I'm slow to figure out I ought to follow it.
Now Mary Norbert Körte
reads a poem mentioning mugwort
and I admonish myself:

For a smart guy, Mister,
you sure are a dumbshit—
no particular kind,
as vague as "wildflower,"
as vague as "shrub" or "herb" or "tree."
You're just a dumbshit
generally.

What Would Be an Elegy, If It Were a Poem

If I were a poet
I would write a poem

The poem would be an elegy
on the death of poetry

I would write about it
like I could write about the death of my grandmother

how I fell to the kitchen floor
as if my bones had been ripped from me

It was like there were two of me
one flopped down on the floor, all meat and blood

the other just a skeleton
bleached white and lifeless

hanging in some biology classroom
after the students and teacher had gone

after the custodian had come through
and turned off the lights

and the only sound
was the gurgling of a fish tank across the room

where a turtle swam back and forth
and then stopped

I used to stare at walls
hoping for a poem to appear

Now that poetry is dead
I just stare at walls

I Envy the Illiterate

I envy the illiterate, sometimes—
the child who barely has the alphabet,
the woodcutter who didn't finish school
& whose home doesn't have a wall or more of books.
What do they write?
Only what a dragged stick pokes into soft earth.

Whales and Jazz

I was asked to give a reading at a festival
Of whales and jazz.
Whales and jazz?
What do I know about whales and jazz? Whales
Or jazz?
What do I know about that wet world
And what of smoky rooms where music blooms?
What do I know of living in one world,
Breathing in another,
Going down and staying down,
Living in hiding 'til I blow my steam,
Wandering homeless, nearly aimless,
Heading for the warmth, for the food,
Of ever searching for my fill?
What do I know of whales, I ask you?
It can't be any more than what I know of jazz,
What I know of mu-sac,
What I know of sounds bubbling up
Of their own accord,
Following their own complex logic,
Of occasional discord,
Of rhythms that vary,
That shimmer and shimmy and sway,
Of finding the groove with my fellow man,
My fellow wo-man,
Of loving the music that we make between us.
What do I know of improvisation,
Of making it up,
Of catch-as-catch-can,
Of wondering what the day will bring,
What the long, dark night will bring,
Wondering where the tune can go,
And seeing it out to the end,

To the last fading note.
What do I know of jazz
Or whales?
Whales and jazz, wailing jazz?
What do I know of the sounds whales make,
Of those slow songs,
Of the loneliness between them,
Of the sound vibrations traveling miles, miles,
Of looking for someone to say something to,
Of hoping they care,
Of hoping they're willing to do some singing, too?
What do I know?
What do I know of whales and jazz,
Of wailing jazz,
Of jazzing up my wailing?
I don't have a saxophone.
I don't have a snaredrum and the
Brushstick-smooth beats.
I did have a trumpet back in 5th grade,
But that was no jazz,
That was no music:
Ber-ber-ber ber-ber-ber...
Oh it was bad,
So bad even I knew my mom's smile
Was holding something back,
Something crucial,
Something definitive,
Something like a jazzman holds back
Waiting for the break,
Waiting for the solo when he's gonna let it all go,
When he hits the surface,
When he really starts to breath,
When he really starts to blow.
Yeah,
What do I know about whales and jazz?
What do I know about peering out into the salty murk,

About wishing I could see farther,
About shapes darting by,
About wondering what's behind me,
Wondering what's ahead,
About listening,
Listening for my brethren,
For my love, for my children,
For my life,
About listening to every beat,
Every squeal
In this world of sound.
What do I know about midnight riffs,
About the darkness around me,
About finding my way,
About making up my own songs
That start slow
And build up in the mystery of their making
To a crescendo
And end eventually in silence?
What do I know?
What do I know? Yeah,
I was asked to give a reading at a festival of
Whales and jazz,
And I turned it down.
I turned it down.
I took my breath and headed back on down
To my own wet world
Of sounds
And silence.
But I'll be back.
A man's gotta breathe.
A man's gotta blow.

Ironed Shirts

I accept this destiny of ironed shirts.
—Julio Cortazar

Oh, Julio, now you have me second-guessing,
wondering if this life, wrinkle-free
& tucked in every day, isn't in some
fundamental way
a screwed up trade off
wherein my time—which is
after all my life—has been sold
to the highest bidder (and not that high either).

Yet I must consider the quality of my life,
the health & happiness of my wife,
& note especially that we're looking
to buy a new house—
& a nice house it will be, too—
"a sanctuary" in my wife's words,
"a place where I can write a poem" in mine.

And yes, I can hear you, Julio—or is it me?—
saying a poem can be written
anywhere—a study isn't needed—
anywhere—trees aren't needed—
or if trees are needed they're available
for free in any public park—
let the taxpayers foot the bill,
let the city's maintenance crew
rake the leaves & water the flowers
& leave me to write my poems—
poems free to be untucked,
fully wrinkled, loose as truth
& wild as a tribe of rabid squirrels.

Revision

We pass a car crumpled and torn
Like a paper ball on the roadside,
Like an old draft of a poem
Revised and alive somewhere else.

Back home, if we ever make it,
I'll take up again a favorite book
Whose cover declares,
You Must Revise Your Life—
A hard line to refute
While staring out a gray window
Through windshield wipers
That wave their warning arms
To the beat of pelting rain.

Headlights slice past me;
Mine slice past them:
Like any gamble
It's a matter of chance
That keeps this car from folding
Itself into another
In what we call an accident.

I think suddenly of boys playing God
In dirt, slamming Hot Wheels
And Matchbox cars,
I think of the how many
Millions or billions
Spent for supercolliders to
Smash together two tiny atoms,
And I think of young lips
Eager to crash into a first kiss.

I feel like the father
Of a young girl
Clutching his fists as he pleads
To the matchmaker moon,
Not yet, not yet. It is not time.

I pull off the road
And look into my wife's eyes.
Cars speed past
Like frantic hands writing left to right.
She has the bluest eyes.

Not everything needs to be revised.

On Becoming Distinguished

I'm slow to think, *Damn,*
I'll never make distinguished poet, somewhere
midway through watching a video of
a couple of at once laurelled and living poets.
I'm too loose with my words
like those parents too lax, too lazy, or
maybe too self-centered to be anything
but lenient to the twerps they birthed.
The video ends, and I'm staring out the back door
from the bed where I sit between
sleeping dog and sleeping wife.
A chipmunk darts along the rock wall I fashioned
loosely to hold a little soil for flowers.
It finds an acorn, then the highest rock for a perch
—as if he were going to give a reading—
and flails through the shell to the meat within.
Hurrying works for some, I see.
Keeping alive is the main thing.

VI

From the beginning, there is no permanence.

—Epic of Gilgamesh

I left the woods for as good a reason as I went there. Perhaps it seemed to me that I had many more lives to live, and could not spare any more time for that one.

—Henry David Thoreau

New Year's Night, San Francisco

He was sitting looking out over the city—
he was dressed in the clothes of the gods.
　　　　—Steven Vincent Benét

The rest of you can go to sleep, I'll stay here,
Two thirds drunk and just shy of
Totally content. It's not often, or ever,
I get to play the one percent and sit up here
Above the world like this. I've read enough
To know we are the gods, these miracles
Are the stuff of magic, and so I'll watch
The sun rise up in a while over this grand city,
A monument to Western brilliance, to human
Ingenuity and creativity. Of course this may be
The end of the gods, this year of 2012,
If the Mayas are to be believed, or those who
Report such insights to the rest of us.
Has anyone checked up on this folk wisdom?
For me it would be enough to reset the calendar
On discovering we aren't alone in all this
Vast blackness, which just now I can hardly see
From all the lights beneath me. Life will
Find a way, I suspect, that it's not just this
Earth that's so hospitable but the whole fine
Spinning expanding starburst universe
We call home, whether it be like the one I will
Return to, with my books and a woodstove
Ready to light, or like this one, walled with
Glass and a view of so much of what makes me
Marvel at, and fear, the prospect of finding
We have neighbors we never knew. Let us
Toast to them and to us all: health, peace,
Safe travels, a happy New Year, and many more.

If We Are a Cancer

If we are a cancer, we are
A beautiful cancer: swift to kill,
Graceful as we overwhelm,
Mixing mountaintop removal
And Stonehenge, the monotony
Of the suburbs and Mozart,
Gang deaths and vivid colors
In graffiti memorials to those slain.
The next Robinson Crusoe
Will be trapped on an island
Of plastic, where on clear nights
He will learn to whistle songs
To the moon that passing humpbacks
Will hear and wish were theirs.
When the last of us goes,
The trees and grasshoppers
And blue jays will be silent
A moment, will sigh together
For relief, and as a lament.
Never was there a more magnificent
Plague upon this gentle earth.

On the Expansion of the Universe

My vote was for the center to reaffirm its hold,
for gravity to bring the big bang back around to crunch,

to the pin-point unity my boyhood hands folded together
hoped to find in this congested, desperate world.

But the jury of scientific journals has fluttered its pages
together long enough to now pronounce its finding,

that all the fuzzy spirals of galaxies—like little twists
of sheep's wool—are wandering farther and farther afield,

that the fence is broken by storm and unmendable,
that the flock is lost, that the shepherd is helpless,

that you and I, even if we weren't going to die,
would drift ever farther apart.

Of course, maybe the shepherd opened the gate.
Let's make the most of our time.

If There Should Be Stones

If there should be stones between us
We could work together
Stacking stone on stone to build a wall
A clean line we'd agree on
And then we could sit and watch moss grow
You on your side
Me on mine

Better yet
We could make a Stonehenge
A megalith, a temple
And we could worship under the moon and stars
Together
Each in our own way

Old Fool

Neither of us is wise enough to understand a moment,
Neither one poet enough to speak convincingly of the
      immortal,

But when we're together we have our laughs,
Strum our guitars, drink our beer, dilly-dally and dawdle

Until you need to go again, and I stand in the driveway
Feeling like an old fool of a mountain hermit—

Friendless, wifeless, without even the dog
Who sighs as your car rounds the distant bend.

To Olaf Palm

On his "Self Portrait at Gravesite"

i

Looking at your mandolin,
the hands that hold it
where you sit on a log in a meadow,
the colors of your sweater
and your warm scarf,
I'm slow to notice the three
gravestones over your right shoulder.
They rise from the grass
like gray tongues,
one in the shape of a cross.
They sing nothing.
You have no accompaniment.

ii

Christian, a friend
who knew you, said by then
you knew the cancer
was unstoppable, that
the gravesite you played for
was your gravesite.
Again my eyes go
to the mandolin, your fingerings,
and the song I hear
doesn't change, exactly, but slows,
slows, slower,
each note hanging like a gull
in the winds above a nearby coastal cliff,

wingspread over waves, soaring
as far as it can, as
long as it can,
knowing
it will have to land,
and learning to live with that.

When You Leave

Every one of my multitudes
Mourns
Every one of your multitudes

Loss is expansive
Exponential

Only the mathematicians of grief
Know where this ends

Will there be time enough

Let the river start with me

Together we will discover
What ocean it finds

In That Irish Graveyard

I fell in love with you again
In that Irish graveyard,
Wandering among the dead,
Finding the vine-entwined
Ruin of a tomb,
Taking your photo, again and again,
While the sun leaned an elbow
On the green hills behind me,
While the lake below us
Meditated on its own stillness.
And all those aged tombstones—
The Celtic crosses, the names and dates—
All those bones buried there
In the cold green earth
Were somehow suddenly all right,
Were celebrations, really,
If those lives had truly lived,
If they too knew this joy,
This peace, this solace, this love.
When I said, "Hold that pose,"
It was like a vow:
I meant forever.

What We Did

When we return to school friends will ask,
What did you do with your summer?

What did we do while the sun spun above the heads
of tourists on Hawaiian beaches, in Mexican pools?

We ate and drank and slept;
we sat and read and slept some more.

We watched oak leaves fall in afternoon breeze
and let our minds follow their slow drift to earth.

The Empty Bowl

Teacher Chaperone, Sendai, Japan

It was the wrong temple,
the wrong stone steps up though
pine tree lines and stone lanterns.
Our temple was further
down the boulevard
and turn right, but unknown to us
then when we took off our shoes
and stepped into the gold statuary,
where candles burned
and statues watched us
peer into dark alcoves and up
at rice paper paintings.
And then the journey was done,
the kids, my wife
on hold because what I did not know
had brought me
brought me suddenly to tears:
a single painting high overhead
of a man in rags
who knelt, broken and exhausted,
and held aloft
with a frail arm
an empty bowl
halfway to the heavens, and I knew
it was the empty bowl
we all seek
to fill.

On a Photo a Student Gave Me Long Ago

When the unruly spectrum of this dizzying life
is tamed, tempered by craft and ingenuity,
by technology and a will to simplify
until only three hues remain,

I suppose it is right, that it is proper,
for the image to be of just one
young person, his face half in shadow,
and that his hand should be bringing to his mouth

water, a simple glass of water.

Fire Walk

Some mornings I am a shaman
    Staring into the fire
    As seasons of the woods pass,
Watching sapling stretch to madrone,
    Feed berries to blue jays,
    Then fall in a violent night storm.

Some mornings the fire I make
    Burns me,
    Turns my slow eyes to ash
And leads me further in
    To the warmth
    Of its dark smoke arms.

There are footsteps in the coals.
Some mornings they are mine.

Wisdom

I could sit up on this mountain
knee-crunched in lotus pose
limp-lidded & loaded on Om
but it wouldn't do any good

I'm too dipshit to make
enlightenment this time around
& wise enough to know it

but I'm also forgetful & still try
every now & then

Not Much

I'm not much
of a mountain hermit,
truth be told.

Kate's always here
to bicker &
giggle with,

& whole days go by
with me still
in my slippers.

The sparrows
feeding beside me
don't seem to mind.

They're easy,
kinder than people,
& let me indulge—

which is why I want
so much to need
so little like them.

Strange Sounds on the Roof

Just waking this morning we wondered
At the strange sounds on the roof
Or outside somewhere—no threat, but
Peculiar. First thoughts, though,
Are not deep inquiries, are closer
To the basics: bed, wife, warm,
And then to worries of coffee
And making a fire in the woodstove.
And it was venturing toward the kitchen
I saw what that sound had been. Snow
Covered the deck, the handrails,
And sagged the branches of the redwoods
Just outside. The world was white,
Unexpectedly, joyously white.
And that's how it is: the divinity,
The illustriousness of this existence
Sneaks up on us when we're not looking,
Wraps our home in its loving embrace
And whispers, "Wake up, wake up!"
This world is a playground, waiting
For us to step out and frolic, for—
No matter what you may have heard—
These are blesséd days.

Thank You

Thank you for my imagination which today
is a porcupine waddling the forest floor,
picking up leaves of autumn,
the long silken hairs of women I've never met,
lingo and laughter that bursts into guffaw,
and an awe, suddenly, for the scent of green.

Thank you for my imagination that transcends today
then veers back on itself, imagining itself imagining itself
like a mirror remembering its reflection,
its reflection, its reflection...
                        Thank you
for my imagination that is a turnip turning in the earth
like the undead buried and scratching its coffin lid,
spinning like a dancer in a little girl's music box
to the pink-pink notes of Twinkle-Twinkle.

Thank you for my imagination, for my little star,
my little spinning secret solar system
with unnamed planets with unmanned moons
and unconcerned arcing orbits
that get what needs to go where there just in time.

Thank you for the tree growing in my vegetable imagination
like a quick weed, an itching need to reach up
and out and find the sun that shines its light
for lord and lad both, for lady, lass and little
but quick-sprouting tree.
                        Thank you
for my imagination, my other me, my better me,
        my freer me.

And thank you for the light toward which I rise.

Folding

Carefully take a few kind words,
Bring them to a point, here.
Lift the corners of the mouth,
Fold them up just so. Good. You are doing well.
Now pull up part of your soul
Over a friend's cold legs. Excellent. Precisely.
Origami.
We are all swans.

And With That, Goodnight

I'm not so stupid I haven't noticed
that the calendar's learning to flip itself faster each month.
And the sun's greased the track, has us spinnin' around it
quicker than a hula-hoop around a twelve year old.

I can hardly get a poem started
before it's time to go to bed.

And I could be dead tomorrow.
Or you.

So I just wanted to point out the white moths
flittering up there in the redwood branches overhead.

They're there. And they're beautiful.

Love Song

As still as a fence post
    As still as a stone
As still as the moon
    Or a buried bone

As still as sculpture
    Or an old soup can
So still do we sleep
    Hand curled in hand

Last Watering

Looking up I saw
Kate at the window watching me
And saw for a moment
Me standing there with the hose in my hand,
Water arcing down to the base
Of the rose bush, in the garden
We planted together, nurtured into green
Abundance over years
That had to eventually end.
This was the last time
I would step along the path
Trimmed with stones I put end to end,
The last time I would hear above me
Those trees massaged by afternoon breeze.
The house is sold, the new owners
Will take over from here.
To them I leave my efforts at stewardship,
At improving the land I claimed
To own, as if land could give itself
Completely to the hand that signed
A small stack of papers.
If we are to find grace in this lifetime,
It is in humbly tending to a piece of land
Like this, not for ourselves,
But to pass on to others,
That they might tend it in their time,
That they might pass it on in turn,
Each of us thankful, each of us
Understanding with a sort of awkward patience
That in this way
We, too, slowly grow.

Notes

FOREWORD

vi. The line by W.S. Merwin (b. 1927) comes from his introduction to a book of Chinese poetry translations, *Crossing the Yellow River*, by Sam Hamill (b. 1942).

PART ONE

1. Li Po (701-762), or Li Bai, was a celebrated poet of the T'ang dynasty, so great he was referred to as The Banished Immortal. The translation is my own, based on others, from the poem alternately called "Mountain Dialogue" and "Question Answered."

1. The Robert Frost (1874-1963) quote, a favorite of mine, is from his poem, "Birches."

6. Redwoods: According to Snopes.com Ronald Reagan has been misquoted, but his actual words, as a gubernatorial candidate speaking to the Western Wood Products Association on March 12th, 1966, were similar in spirit: "We've got to realize that where the preservation of a natural resource like the redwoods is concerned, that there is a common sense limit...you know, a tree is a tree, how many more do you need to look at?" A year later, on March 15th, in reference to the oldest of redwoods he said, "I saw them; there is nothing beautiful about them, just that they are a little higher than the others."

18. Four Seasons Fast: At some point in 2008, the TB Greene Gallery in Ukiah had a display of local haiku, beautifully framed and downright respectable. These were among them. The gallery folded soon after....

19. Geraniums: The quote, or epigraph, is from the Talking Heads song, "Same as It Ever Was."

26. The Way of Water: This was written after the death of a friend, Dori Anderson, on January 4, 2008. A Ukiah librarian, she was also a co-founder of the ukiaHaiku Festival (with Susan Sparrow) and a faithful member of the Ukiah Poet Laureate Committee. In verse 66 of the *Tao Te Ching*, Lao Tzu (sixth century BC) writes,

"The reason the sea can govern a hundred rivers
is because it has mastered being lower."

PART TWO

27. The haiku is by Kobayashi Issa (1763-1828), one of the most revered of all Japanese poets. Written after the death of one of his children, this little poem wrestles with the Buddhist idea of the world as illusion. In his phrase "and yet" is all the beauty, and suffering, of our lives. The translation is by Robert Hass.

27. The quote by German poet Rainer Maria Rilke (1875-1926) is from a letter written November 18th, 1920.

29. The Starlings of Cloverdale: The quote by Wallace Stevens (1879-1955) is from his poem, "Final Soliloquy of the Interior Paramour."

30. Tickling Her to Sleep: Chuang Tzu (369–286 BC?), along with Lao Tzu, is one of the great masters of Taoism.

42. Emails to Tonya: This was written after the passing of our friend and colleague Tonya Sparkes. See Hayden Carruth's (1922-2008) "Faxes to William" in his book *Scrambled Eggs & Whiskey* for my model. The quote from Emily Dickinson (1830-1886) is from her poem #96, "My life closed twice before its close."

46. "Love's Austere and Lonely Offices": This title comes from the last line of a poem written by Robert Hayden (1913-1980), "Those Winter Sundays."

PART THREE

49. The short quote by John Ashbery (b. 1927) is from his poem, "Sacred and Profane Dances."

49. The Robinson Jeffers (1887-1962) quote is from his poem, "Shine, Perishing Republic."

54. Lorca's Body: This was written after reading an article about the Spanish poet Federico Garcia Lorca (1898-1936) in the *New Yorker*, "Looking for Lorca." December 22, 2003. He was murdered by a firing squad of Franco's forces at the onset of the Spanish Civil War. As of the publication of this book, his remains have yet to be exhumed.

56. WestPoint: Wilfred Owen (1893-1918), an English soldier widely considered the finest poet of World War I, ended his very well anthologized poem, "Dulce Et Decorum Est," with this Latin phrase (taken from an ode by Horace) which translates as "It is sweet and right to die for your country." He was shot and killed on November 4th, 1918, and his parents received the telegram as bells rang on Armistice Day a week later.

64. Forgetting the World: Han Shan, whose name means "Cold Mountain," is the archetypal poet-recluse of T'ang dynasty China.

PART FOUR

67. The Jane Hirshfield (b. 1953) quote is taken from her essay, "Poetry as a Vessel of Remembrance."

67. Emily Dickinson's (1830-1886) quote is from her poem #1129, "Tell All the Truth."

69. Five Tanka on a Trip to Japan I Have Yet to Take: Tanka are a haiku-like 5 line Japanese poem. Matsuo Bashō (1644-1694) is Japan's most famous haiku poet. These were written in anticipation of the trip to Japan we did later take.

80. Self-Portrait by Vincent Van Gogh: (1853-1890) The particular self-portrait I have in my classroom is a very dark one titled, *Self-Portrait, 1887-88,* (F1672a).

89. The Curtains: The quote is from Polish poet Jerzy Jarniewicz (b. 1958) from his prose poem, "Leaving the City."

92. Lines Written Just Before Nothing Occurred: This villanelle is written in the voice of Harold Camping, the false prophet who was sure he knew the time and date of the rapture. In the same spirit—if a little less harsh—the next poem, the loosely ending sonnet called A Humble Prophecy (p. 93), is my also failed attempt to put a date on the future—2012. Yeah, well.

96. My Nine Horses: See the cover of Billy Collins's (b. 1941) book, *Nine Horses,* and my poem will make sense. Read his book, and the tone of my poem might also make sense.

100. The Ballad of Black Bart and the Irish Lass: This was written on the day after arriving home from our trip to Ireland. I later read the fine book, *Black Bart: Boulevardier Bandit: The Saga of California's Most Mysterious Stagecoach Robber and the Men Who Sought to Capture Him.* I recommend it for those wanting genuine facts.

PART FIVE

105. The Marianne Moore (1887-1972) quote is from her poem, "Poetry," which goes from this rough introduction to admitting, "however, with a perfect contempt for it, one discovers in/ it after all, a place for the genuine."

105. The Jane Kenyon (1947-1995) quote is from her essay, "Thoughts on the Gifts of Art."

107. First Thought: One of the greatest responses I've ever received about a poem was Jim Lyle's huge laughter when I read this one night in Willits. A fine poet himself, Jim Lyle (b. 1931) is a generous supporter of younger writers.

108. My Prelude: Colleen, my older sister, took me book shopping when I was 18 or 19. The quote is from T. S. Eliot's (1888-1965) "Preludes." The slim volume she bought me, *The Wasteland and Other Poems*, was one of the books that changed my life. I will forever be grateful.

112. Famous: The Ezra Pound (1885-1972) quote comes from "In Epitaphium," which reads in its entirety:

> "Write me when this geste, our life is done:
> He tired of fame before the fame was won."

114. My Library: Mark Strand (b. 1934) quote is from his poem, "Eating Poetry."

115. Kerouac's *Book of Haikus*: All titles are by Jack Kerouac (1922-1969). Japhy is character in *Dharma Bums* and is based on the poet Gary Snyder (see below).

116. Bixby Canyon: See the novel *Big Sur* by Jack Kerouac.

117. Mugwort: The Gary Snyder (b. 1930) quote is from his poem, "To the Children." Mary Norbert Körte (b. 1934), one of the preeminent poets in Northern California—at the very least—, is a tremendous inspiration to all who hear her read.

123. Ironed Shirts: The quote by Julio Cortazar (1914-1984) is from his poem "The Good Boy" from the book, *Saving Twilight*, translated by Gualala poet Stephen Kessler (b. 1947).

124. Revision: The title in my poem is a book by William Stafford (1914-1993) about writing and the teaching of poetry.

PART SIX

127. The Gilgamesh quote is from Tablet X, Column VI, 32, of the great Sumerian epic, which dates back to the third millennium BC. The translation is by John Gardner and John Maier.

127. The Henry David Thoreau (1817-1862) quote is from *Walden*'s final chapter, "Conclusion."

129.   New Year's Night, San Francisco: The quote is from the short story, "By the Waters of Babylon" by Stephen Vincent Benét (1898-1943). A tribal man discovers the remains of a god in the high-rise ruins he calls the City of the Gods and learns it was a man who had watched the destruction of old New York City.

134. To Olaf Palm: Olaf Palm (1935-2000), who lived on the Mendocino coast, was an astounding painter "trained in the traditional techniques of the Dutch and Flemish masters."

136. When You Leave: Walt Whitman (1819-1892), in section 51 of "Song of Myself" writes, "I contain multitudes." He does, and we all do.

Acknowledgements

Thanks, first of all, to my family, whose support through the years has helped make me the man I am. Special thanks go to my Lita—my dad's mother—who, more than anyone, has shown me that art and beauty are around us always, that they are ways of living in the world.

Thanks to the Monday writing group who first heard and inspired some of these poems: Christopher Douthit, Rosemary Eddy, Ronald K. Ford, Kathryn McInnis, Kay Spencer, and a shifting cast of other friends.

Thanks to those who support the poetry scene around Mendocino County, organizing readings where a good majority of these poems made their early debuts: Mike A'Dair, Dan Barth, Gordon Black, Bill Bruneau, Jabez Churchill, John Koetzner, blake more, David Partch, Dan Roberts, Susan Sparrow & Hal Zina Bennett of Tenacity Press, Theresa Whitehill, and many others.

Thanks, also, to Dan Barth and Christopher Douthit for their diligent proofreading and advice during the making of this book.

Of course, I owe no one greater thanks than Kate, my wife, my guide, my first and toughest editor, my best friend, my love. Thank you eternally.

Michael Riedell was born and raised in San Diego County and currently lives in Ukiah, California. A writer of poems and songs, he has had work featured in national poetry magazines as large as the *Lilliput Review* and *Brevities*, and in a regional anthology, *Small Mirrors*. He is a three-time first place winner of the ukiaHaiku contest, has long been a member of the Ukiah Poet Laureate Committee, and now helps judge the ukiaHaiku contest. He spends his days teaching adolescents the correct uses of semicolons and the collective wisdom of the Western Canon; at night he strums guitar and sings to the chagrin of both his wife, Kate, and their hypercritical canine, Kona the Wonder Dog.

Goudy Old Style is an old-style classic sarif typeface originally created by Frederic W. Goudy in 1915. Generally classified as a Garalde face, certain of its attributes—most notably the gently curved, rounded serifs of certain glyphs—suggest a Venetian influence. Goudy Old Style is considered to be among the most legible and readable serif typefaces for use in print applications.